Air

At Heron Books, we think learning should be engaging and fun. It should be hands-on and it should allow students to move at their own pace.

For this purpose, we have created an accompanying learning guide to help the student progress through this book, chapter by chapter, with increasing confidence, interest and independence.

Get your free learning guide at *heronbooks.com/learningguides*.

For a final exam, email *teacherresources@heronbooks.com*.

We would love to hear from you!
Email us at *feedback@heronbooks.com*.

Published by
Heron Books, Inc.
20950 SW Rock Creek Road
Sheridan, OR 97378

heronbooks.com

Special thanks to all the teachers and students who provided feedback instrumental to this edition.

Fourth Edition © 1976, 2018, Heron Books
All Rights Reserved

ISBN: 0-89739-103-9

Any unauthorized copying, translation, duplication or distribution, in whole or in part, by any means, including electronic copying, storage or transmission, is a violation of applicable laws.

Printed in the USA

22 November 2018

IN THIS BOOK

1 AIR IS ALL AROUND YOU 3
    Chapter 1 Activities 4

2 AIR IN MANY PLACES 9
    Chapter 2 Activities 13

3 AIR TAKES UP SPACE 17
    Chapter 3 Activities 19

4 AIR HAS WEIGHT 25
    Chapter 4 Activity 26

5 AIR AS WIND 29
    Chapter 5 Activities 30
        Make A Pinwheel 30
        Make A Sailboat 32
        Make A Parachute 34

6 AIR PUSHES 39
Chapter 6 Activities 44

7 THINGS YOU KNOW ABOUT AIR 49
Chapter 7 Activities 50

Chapter 1

Air Is All Around You

Air Is All Around You

Air is all around you. You can feel air moving when you blow on your hand. You can feel air moving when you breathe.

When you run, you push against the air and can feel it. You walk through air whenever you move. When you blow up a balloon, you are putting air into it.

If you pop the balloon, the air rushes out. You cannot see air, but you can feel it, and you can see what it does.

There is air all around you.

CHAPTER 1 ACTIVITIES

1. Go outside and run fast. Feel the air as you move.

2. Get a straw and blow through it at another person. See if he or she feels the air.

3. Take the straw and blow through it at someone's hair. Watch what happens.

4. Get a glass of water and a straw. Put the straw into the water and blow through it. Watch what happens.

5. Get a balloon and blow into it. Tell your teacher why you think the balloon gets larger when you blow into it. Keep the balloon for the next step.

6. Blow up a balloon really big. Get help tying it if you need to. Take a pin and stick it into the balloon.

7. Talk to your teacher about what happens and what air has to do with this.

Chapter 2

Air in Many Places

Air in Many Places

2

There is air in soil. **Soil** is made up of tiny pieces of rock and wood and other things. The little spaces between the pieces of rock and wood and other things are filled with air.

AIR IN MANY PLACES

Did you know that there is even air in some rocks? There is a kind of rock called pumice. **Pumice** is a light rock with many holes in it. There is air in the holes in pumice.

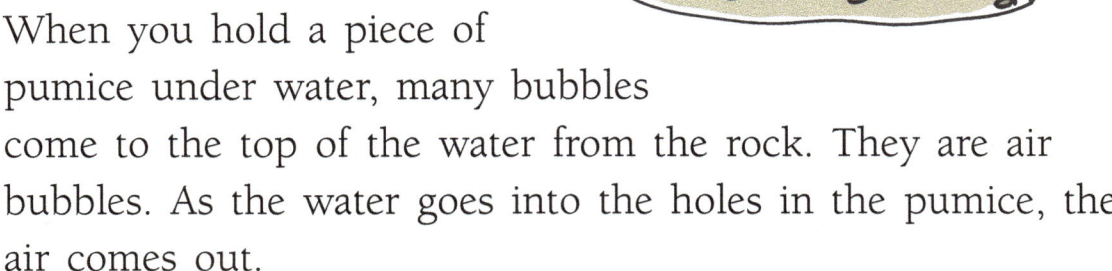

When you hold a piece of pumice under water, many bubbles come to the top of the water from the rock. They are air bubbles. As the water goes into the holes in the pumice, the air comes out.

A sponge has air in it. A sponge has holes, like pumice, and there is air in these holes. When you put a sponge in water and squeeze it, bubbles come out of it. These bubbles are air bubbles.

There is air in water. If you fill a glass with water and let it sit for a while, you will see bubbles on the sides of the glass. Air is coming out of the water in these bubbles.

AIR IN MANY PLACES

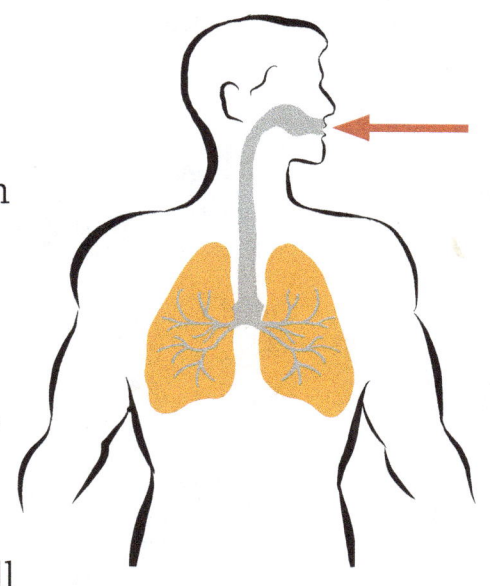

There are spaces inside your body filled with air. Air gets into your ears and nose. When you open your mouth to eat, air goes in with the food. And when you burp, some of it comes out!

Every time you breathe in (inhale), you take air into a part of your body called the lungs. Your body needs air to live. You breathe air all the time.

Mammals, like cows, dogs and cats, need air. Pigs, horses, and bears need air. These animals have lungs, which the air goes into when they breathe. Animals everywhere must have air to live.

AIR IN MANY PLACES

Even earthworms in the ground need air. They breathe the air in the little spaces in the soil.

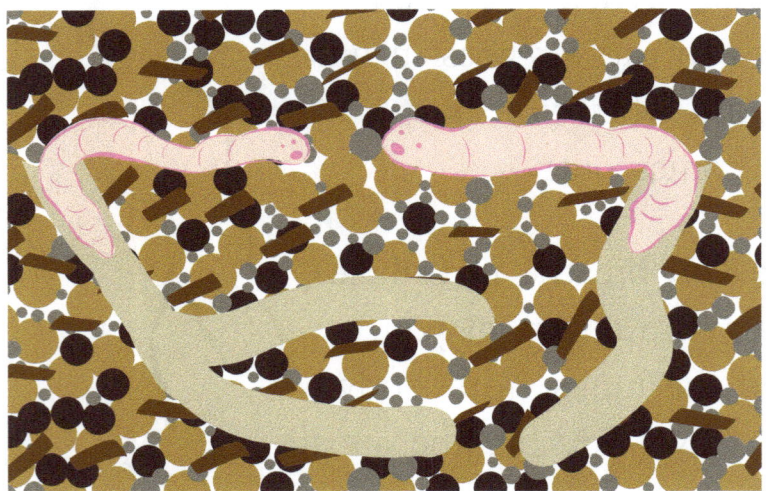

There is air all around us that we breathe and animals breathe.

There is air in soil and some rocks. There is air in a sponge. There is air in water.

There is air almost everywhere!

CHAPTER 2 ACTIVITIES

1. Get a can or a pan and fill it completely with dry soil. Don't push the soil down. Do you think anything else could fit in the can? Put the filled can in a sink. Now fill a pitcher with water and slowly pour it on the soil. Watch what happens. How could the water fit? Did you see any air bubbles?

2. Get a piece of pumice. Fill a bowl with water and put the pumice in it. Watch what happens. (Save your bowl of water for the next activity.)

3. Get a sponge. Hold the sponge down in the bowl of water. Squeeze it while it is under water. Notice what is in the bubbles that come out of the sponge as you squeeze it.

4. Fill a clear bottle halfway with water. Put it in the refrigerator until it is cold. Take it out, put the lid on the bottle and shake it for a minute. Then put it in a warm place and loosen the lid. After the bottle warms up you should see bubbles in the water. Talk to your teacher about what you observed.

Chapter 3

Air Takes Up Space

Air Takes Up Space 3

Air takes up space. If you see a glass on a table with no water or milk or anything to drink in it, you may think it is empty. The glass seems to be empty, *but is it really empty?*

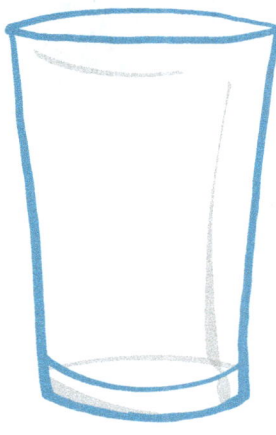

No, the glass is not empty. The glass is full. It is full of air. You cannot see the air, but it fills the glass.

You already know air fills spaces in your body, in soil, and in some rocks. Spaces all around you are filled with air. If there is air in a space, there cannot be water in that space at the same time. The air has to go out of the space before the water can go in.

AIR TAKES UP SPACE

Air does not always take up the same amount of space. When air is heated, it tries to spread out and take up more space. When air is cooled, it tries to come together and take up less space.

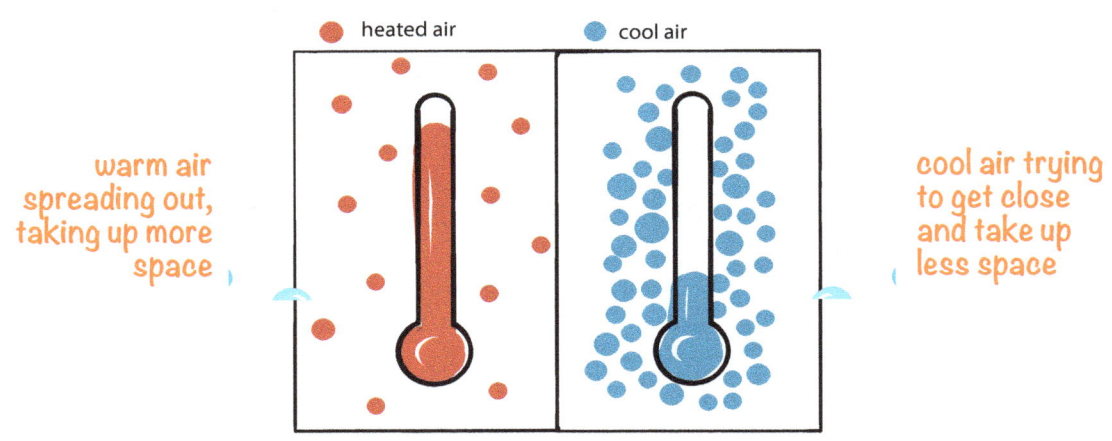

Air takes up space.
It tries to take up more space when it is heated and less space when it is cooled.

CHAPTER 3 ACTIVITIES

1. Fill up a pan with water. Take an empty glass, turn it straight upside down and put it into the pan of water. Tilt it a little. See what comes out. Draw a picture that shows the glass and what came out. Show this drawing to your teacher.

2. Get an empty, dry glass. Push a crumpled piece of paper towel into the bottom of the glass so it stays there when you turn the glass upside down. Decide if you think the paper will get wet if you put the glass upside down in a pan of water.

   Now get a pan of water. Take the glass with the paper in it and holding it straight upside down, push it into the water in the pan. Take it out and pull the paper out of the glass. Feel it and see if it is wet.

19

3. Write a short story that tells what happened. Explain how air takes up space. Show this to your teacher.

4. Blow up a balloon.

   Get a piece of string and have your teacher show you how to measure the balloon. Use a marker to show where you measured.

   Put the balloon inside a refrigerator.

   After ten minutes, take it out and quickly measure it again in the same place. See if there is any difference in the size of the balloon.

   Talk to your teacher about what happened and how cold air takes up less space than warm air.

5. Get a pan of water, a hotplate (a small stove burner), a dish of ice cubes, a balloon, and a glass bottle with a top small enough to fit the balloon over.

With your teacher's help, put the balloon over the top of the bottle. Put the bottle in the pan of water and heat it up on the hot plate. See what happens to the balloon.

Use something to protect your hands such as a hot pad and take the bottle out of the water. Put it in the dish of ice cubes. Now see what happens to the balloon. Talk to your teacher about what happened and why.

Chapter 4

Air Has Weight

Air Has Weight

Air has weight. The more air you put in an object, the heavier the object is. When something is filled with air, it is heavier than when it is almost empty.

A balloon full of air weighs more than a balloon that has little air in it.

A ball filled with air weighs more than a ball with little air in it.

Air does have weight.

CHAPTER 4 ACTIVITY

Get a yardstick and some string. Have someone help you tie one end of the string to something in the room and the other end to the middle of the yardstick, so the stick hangs straight across.

Blow up two balloons so they are very full and tie the ends. Hang one at each end of the stick with tape or string. Move the string on the yardstick until the stick stays straight across with the balloons on it.

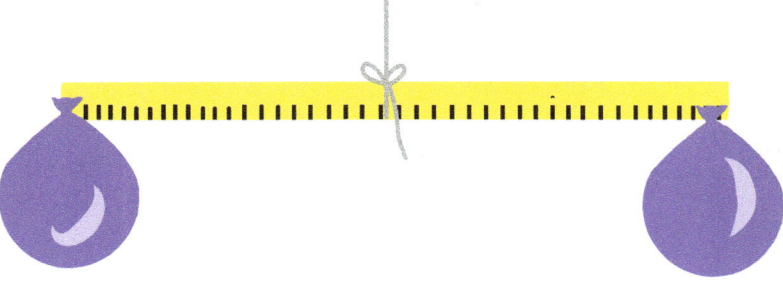

Get a pin. You are going to stick it in one of the balloons carefully so it does not "pop" into many pieces. You want the balloon to stay in one piece.

Stick your pin in one of the balloons. See what happens to the stick the balloons are hanging on.

Do the balloons weigh the same now? Which balloon is heavier? Why?

Tell your teacher the answers to these questions.

Chapter 5

Air As Wind

Air As Wind

Wind is moving air. Wind can move things.

Wind can bend trees.

Wind can make flags fly.

Sailboats move because of wind.

Wind helps kites fly.

There are many ways you can use wind to help you.

CHAPTER 5 ACTIVITIES

MAKE A PINWHEEL

A pinwheel is something that uses moving air, or wind, to make it move. To make a pinwheel, do this:

1. Get a pencil with an eraser, a straight pin, scissors, and a square piece of paper three inches long on each side.

2. Cut the paper like this: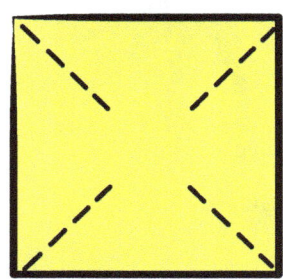

3. Now make a little x on the corners of the paper just like the picture shows.

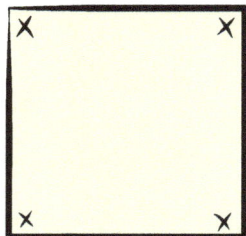

4. Fold the parts with the x's on them into the middle of the paper and hold the ends.

5. Then, where the dot is in the picture, stick the straight pin through the paper so it holds all the ends together.

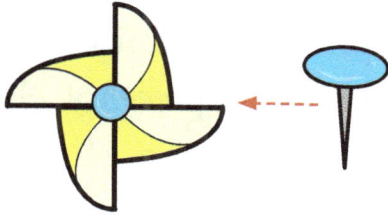

6. Next, take the pin and stick the end into the eraser of the pencil, like this:

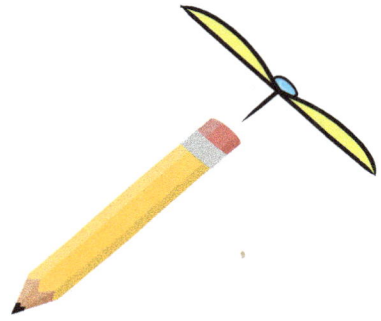

Now you have a pinwheel. Blow on it from the side and see what happens.

MAKE A SAILBOAT

A sailboat uses wind to move. To make a sailboat, do this:

1. Get one square piece of aluminum foil five inches long on each side and a piece of clay. Also, get a toothpick and a square piece of paper two inches long on each side.

2. Take the paper and stick the toothpick through it, like this:

3. Now, take the big piece of aluminum foil and shape it into a boat, like this:

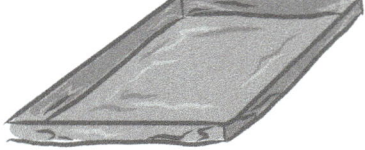

4. Then, take a piece of clay and stick it in the middle of your boat so it will stay.

5. Now, take your sail and push one end of the toothpick into the clay, so the sail stays in place. Now, you have a sailboat!

6. Get a big pan of water and put your sailboat in it. Blow on the sail of your boat. See what happens.

7. Write down on a piece of paper what the wind does here and give the paper to your teacher.

MAKE A PARACHUTE

A parachute uses air and wind to work.

To make a parachute, do this:

1. Get one square of tissue, a spool of thread and a paper clip.

2. Cut off four pieces of thread, each six inches long.

3. Tie each thread onto a corner of the tissue, like this:

4. Now, take the ends of the thread, pull them all together, and tie them.

5. Last of all, tie the ends of the thread to the paper clip.

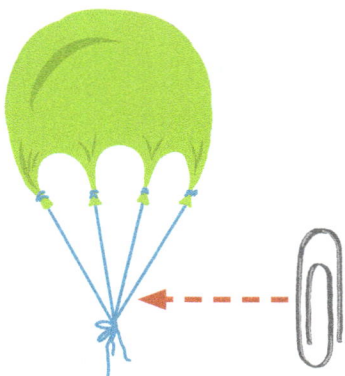

6. Take your parachute, stand on a chair and drop it. Do this five times.

7. Get a fan and turn it on. Hold your parachute in front of the fan and let it go. Do this five times.

8. Talk to your teacher about what air and wind have to do with a parachute working.

Chapter 6

Air Pushes

Air Pushes

Because air has weight, it pushes, or presses, in every direction. It presses up, down, in and out. Air presses on walls, people, books and water. It presses on everything on earth, in all directions.

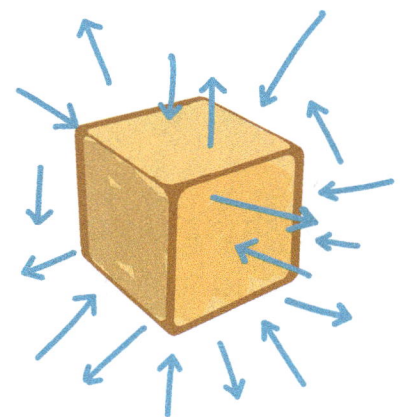

A paper plane can fly because air pushes over the top and bottom of the wings as it moves through the air.

The pressing of air is called **air pressure**.

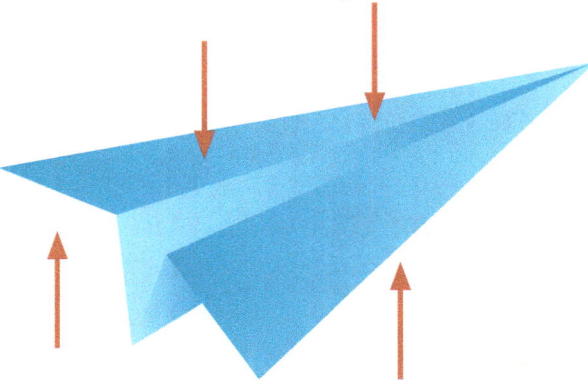

AIR PUSHES

As you blow air into a balloon, the air presses out on the balloon and it begins to get big.

Air can push hard enough to move things. If you put a paper bag under a book and blow it up with air, the book will move.

Air can press harder in one direction than another direction. This can make things happen that seem strange.

You can fill a glass to the top with water and put a card on top of the glass. Then hold the card in place and turn the glass upside down.

If you take your hand away from the card, the card stays on the bottom of the glass and the water doesn't fall out.

AIR PUSHES

Why does the water stay in the glass?

The card and the water are held up by air pressure. The air presses up on the card and the water. The upward pressure of the air is greater than the downward pressure of the water. So, the card and the water will not fall. There is no air inside the glass to press down.

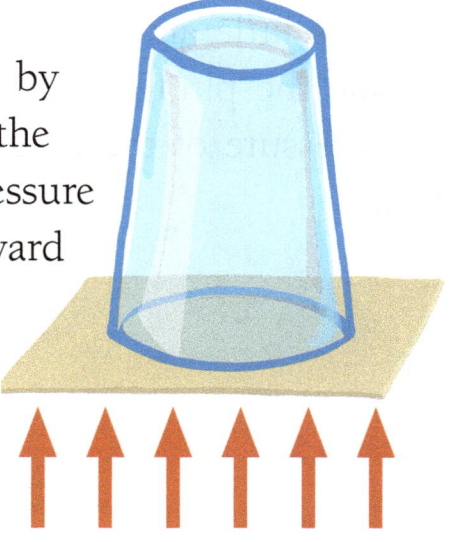

You can take a plunger and push it hard against the wall, like this:

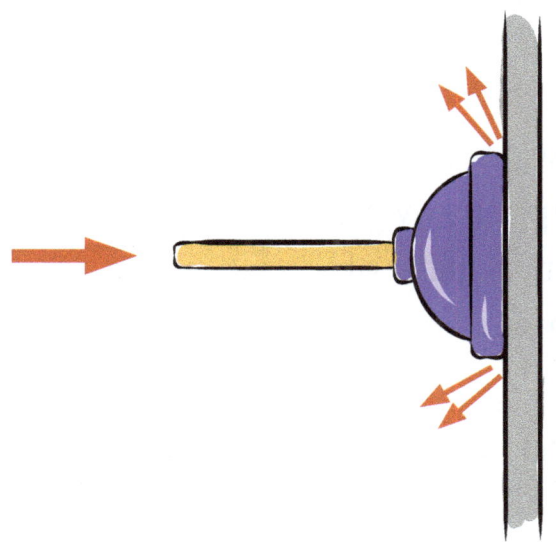

AIR PUSHES

When you do this, the air is pushed out of the plunger. There is little air inside the plunger, so the air pressure outside the plunger is greater than the air pressure inside. The pressure of the outside air holds the plunger on the wall.

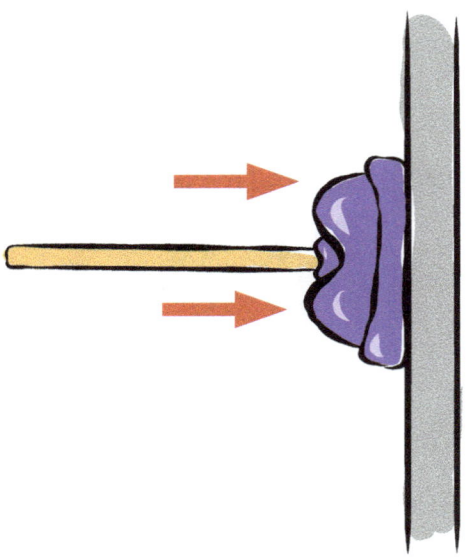

When you use a straw to drink, the same sort of thing happens. When you just set a straw in a glass of water, nothing happens.

AIR PUSHES

Air outside the straw is pushing down on the water. Air inside the straw is pushing down on the water. The water doesn't move.

But when you suck on the straw, you pull some of the air out of the straw.

There is less air in the straw pushing down on the water. The air outside the straw is still pushing down on the water. It pushes hard enough to push some of the water up the straw.

Now, you have learned some things about air pressure and how it works.

Air pushes in all directions and that is called air pressure.

CHAPTER 6 ACTIVITIES

1. Breathe in (inhale) deeply. Now, breathe out (exhale). Do this again. See if your chest gets larger when you inhale and smaller when you exhale.

2. Get a paper bag. Put the paper bag on a table with the opening of the bag over the edge of the table. Put a small book on part of the bag. Blow hard into the bag. See what happens.

3. Do this in a sink or over a pan. Get a glass and a small piece of cardboard. Fill the glass right to the top with water. Put the cardboard on top of the glass. Hold the cardboard with one hand and turn the glass straight upside down. Now, take your hand away from the cardboard. See what happens. Tell your teacher what happened and talk about why that happened.

4. Get a rubber plunger from the teacher. Have the teacher help you push it hard against a flat wall so it sticks. Talk to your teacher about what makes the plunger stay on wall.

5. Get two rubber plungers. You hold one and have another student hold one. Hold them up against each other so they are even and push them together. Try to pull them apart. See what happens.

6. Get a straw and a glass of water. Put the straw in the water. See what happens. Now, suck slowly on the straw. See what happens. Draw a picture of what is happening with the air and the water. Give it to your teacher.

Chapter 7

Things You Know About Air

Things You Know About Air   7

Now you know air is around you almost everywhere.

You know air takes up space. It tries to take up more space when it is heated and less space when it is cooled.

You know air has weight.

You know air as wind can move things.

And you know air pushes in all directions, and that is called air pressure.

There is so much to know about air!

CHAPTER 7 ACTIVITIES

1. Use what you have learned about air to make two toys or things that use air to make them work.

2. Go tell a grown-up all you have learned about air. Show the toys or things you made and explain how these work with air.

www.ingramcontent.com/pod-product-compliance
Lightning Source LLC
Chambersburg PA
CBHW050504110426
42742CB00018B/3372